WEST

WEST

Kenneth Steven

wild goose
publications

www.**ionabooks**.com

Copyright © 2018 Kenneth Steven

First published 2019

Wild Goose Publications
21 Carlton Court, Glasgow G5 9JP, UK
www.ionabooks.com
Wild Goose Publications is the publishing division of the Iona Community.
Scottish Charity No. SC003794. Limited Company Reg. No. SC096243.

ISBN 978-1-84952-640-1

Cover and internal photographs © Kristina Hayward

Overseas distribution:
Australia: Willow Connection Pty Ltd, Unit 4A, 3-9 Kenneth Road,
Manly Vale, NSW 2093
New Zealand: Pleroma, Higginson Street, Otane 4170, Central Hawkes Bay
Canada: Novalis/Bayard Publishing & Distribution, 10 Lower Spadina Ave.,
Suite 400, Toronto, Ontario M5V 2Z2

Printed by Bell & Bain, Thornliebank, Glasgow

MIX
Paper from
responsible sources
FSC
www.fsc.org
FSC® C007785

CONTENTS

INTRODUCTION

It seems like yesterday, but it was actually more than 20 years ago, when Helen Steven – then Peace and Justice worker for the Iona Community – handed me a manuscript. It contained some writing by her younger brother. 'I think it's rather good,' she said. 'I'd be interested in your opinion.'

It certainly was good. Helen's brother was only 14 or so at the time, and his writing style greatly impressed me. I wrote to tell him so.

Now while it would be somewhat disingenuous of me to claim that I launched Kenneth Steven on his road to literary distinction, I do take a certain satisfaction in witnessing the burgeoning of a deserved reputation among his peers. Nowadays, Kenneth is regarded as one of Scotland's finest poets and prose writers, gaining excellent reviews for his work. His admirers have included the late Poet Laureate Ted Hughes.

I'm not surprised that Helen Steven was so proud of her brother's work. Helen, who died on April 12 at the age of 73, is fondly remembered as an inspirational worker for justice and peace. A passionate campaigner against weapons of mass destruction, she and her partner Ellen Moxley won the respect not just of supporters of her cause but of opponents.

Kenneth Steven recently came up to Orkney to conduct workshops on poetry and creative writing. Twenty-odd years on, I was the pupil and he was the master, and I was right glad. Kenneth is a poet Scotland can be proud of. I am glad to commend WEST, his latest collection.

Let's give him the last word, this gem of a poem titled *Prayer*, from his collection IONA.

If you do not believe in God
Go on a blue spring day across these fields:
Listen to the orchids, race the sea, scent the wind.
Come back and tell me it was all an accident
A collision of blind chance
In the empty hugeness of space.

Ron Ferguson
Writer, journalist and former Leader of the Iona Community

FOREWORD

WEST begins and ends as a song of love to Kenneth Steven's sister Helen, a beloved friend, colleague, fellow-member of the Iona Community and inspirational peace campaigner to many, including me. But the book is also a love story about place. It takes us into the west; to the Atlantic coast of Scotland and its islands, to the far west of Ireland, even into the west-north of Norway and Greenland. The poems are full of shining images of land and sea, and of echoes of the people who once lived in these wild and remote places; a potent reminder of the history in our geographies. The poet writes

I have gone into a landscape
not to come back different
but more myself. It can take days
to go into the hills and listen.

WEST is an enticement to its readers to do the same.

Kathy Galloway
Co-Leader of the Iona Community

MY SISTER HELEN

She was Scotland to me:
bedtime stories that woke me
to the history of Wallace and Bruce,
would have had me up in a saddle,
galloping back in time
for the bits of the border we'd lost.

She lived down endless long windings of bumps,
in cottages with attics and owls –
the hope of conkers in the morning.

She drove me one August night
when the skies were orange and bruised,
till the storm was flickering booms
and we came home in silvering rain.

She was drives at high speed
down roads that should have closed long ago,
in cars that were held together
by the hope of a better tomorrow.

She could conjure a whole ceilidh
out of a candle and an old bothy;
she was songs and tin whistles
in the middle of the worst of blizzards.

She was a beach where you could always swim,
and a place you'd not known before;
she was a fire that would set you alight –
an adventure that was yet to be planned.

MORNING

A band of blood
above the hills that lie in the window;
a straggle of geese limping the windless air,
voices sharp and high.

And now the blue sky clouding grey
and a single boat set in the glass sea –
nothing more: quiet vast, so undisturbed,
it might be the world's first morning.

WEST

Leave Craignure and the woods around Duart Castle
and hug the shore before you climb the lion-coloured hills:
Glen Gorm, from which the people once were burned.
Up higher and still higher, until the lochs lie far below
and if you're lucky, the whole bald head of Ben More
has broken out of cloud and stares west, a weathered sphinx.
A telephone box, a single house, and miles of salt marsh
for the constant hope of otters. Then on, to Pennyghael,
and the thin single road that winds like a piece of thread
over to the cliffs of Carsaig. But keep on heading west,
until Bunessan and the harbour and the clustered houses.
You're almost there. An inland loch, impossibly blue,
and now the breeze blows every way at once –
the land lies low, left with a few wind-twisted trees,
and see, ahead, there, on the edge of the sky,
the island still at anchor; the abbey nestled by the sea –
guarding, keeping, waiting.

AT LAST

It was then that morning
he saw and understood
what it meant, what all this meant;
to be caught here in a place of brokenness –
the rubble of the rocks, the useless lochans,
the unarable land, the relentless days
when there was no going out, no respite;
that it was about this, the wonder of all this,
taking the whole heart hostage.

FORECAST

You can never tell the weather
here in the west. Under the dawn
a lochan is filled unbearably bright,
when all the hills above are lost in mist.
The rusty voices of geese descend
in a veil of rain, and yet
the sun's still somewhere up above –
muffled and struggling. And on a day
the radio tells you to go nowhere at all
because storm's coming thundering in,
the island lies like a gem in a brooch –
not breathing, the sea glass and the air so sweet
you can hear a skylark twirling songs
a whole half mile away.

THERE

Light is only in the field sometimes –
often it is not there at all
and the rain seeps into the corners of the sky
to make the trees that stand between
seem darker, larger than they really are.

When light fills the field
it is like liquid gold filling full a cup,
sometimes so bright the eye
can hardly bear to hold there.

Only once have I known such light
open like a flower so that I was drenched
in all of heaven pouring over me,
until I knew that I stood somewhere
that was mine and no-one else's
for a second, for a moment, for a breath –

that I became a kind of gold
and all the world in shadow lay beyond.

IF

He would have made parables
about corncrakes and larks.

His friends crofters, their bread brought
from the poor fields above the shore.

He would have known Gaelic –
its shapes like a kind of working in wood.

His coming back after three days
like daybreak over the whole ocean.

KILNINVER

On a day of apples and snow
they came down to Kilninver
with the body of the king.

Three days to cross Scotland:
swollen rivers and frozen nights,
the long sadness of a wolf.

And down in Kilninver a nestling
of oaks and river held in the hills' hands.
The sea breathed and shrank, breathed and shrank;
the mountains of Mull with their shoulders of snow.

They slept in a huddle under the oaks,
woke to the firing of starlight
and new snow falling from a sky
that was quieter than silence.

The king held in the vessel,
eyes closed on forty years of war and famine.
They searched the sky for signs,
saw nothing but the flight of a raven right overhead.

And so the boat opened the ice of the water;
they rowed and sea pearls scattered the oars.
Not a word uttered until the island
and the boat was beached at last;
dawn a bonfire burning at their backs.

A child ran down and froze,
sunlight reddening its cheeks, as though understanding.
The people, poor things hunched in cold,
knew to hide their faces.

And so they carried him, high and proud, on his final journey.

THIS LANGUAGE

Even now, so long after the motorway and the wire
have torn tranquillity, it is worth coming here

to listen. But if you really want to understand this language,
you must throw away the rules

forget all you thought you knew –
begin again. Open the book of the moorland

read what is written there in the morning by the mist,
trace with your finger the runes of the birds.

Go and hear the water in the wood as it splays downhill
cold as Greenland. Wait by your window

as the larks on the edge of summer rise and rise,
singing. This land is not for sale –

this language takes a life to learn.

POSTCARD FROM COLONSAY

It was the last day of March;
the wind lifted and thick flocks of snow
filled the air, turned the islands white.

The first lambs out on the hillsides
bewildered and shivering in the blade of spring –
their cries high and helpless.

There was no boat today:
the sea is beside itself, searching and searching
for something it never will find.

THE LOCH

After a long walk into landscape
everything went back to being remote:
the loch impossibly blue and a sandy shore
washed with fragments of wood gnarled to white ghosts.
My mother fished. I hear still the sizzle of the reel
and see the flies blown out on the wind;
how she stood and cast so they danced
on silvering water. I remember chasing
a cloud of damselflies, and red-throated divers –
the ancient echo of their song.
We were above the real world,
held in the hands of the hills,
and yet this mattered more than motorways –
this place bigger and more real
than all we'd left below:
undamaged, undisturbed and undenied.

MOMENT

When the land is rusting
and the wind's come back
to ruffle the trees so it's cold and sore
under the eyes, and the sun
comes but seldom and when it does,
the sea is flooded but above the sky's
left dark and angry.

Then head against the wind
and walk until you have stopped thinking
of all you've left behind, the tasks
that still need doing. You are blown out,
have gone beyond all clocks and watches
into a place where only being matters.

No-one has seen the world through your eyes before
and you stop, breathless, to be given
the moment whooper swans come down as soft as silk
across the surface of a loch
and just above the hills the low moon's
like a ball of cobwebs in the ice-blue skies
and you know, without a doubt,
there could not be anything
so beautiful again.

JUNE

Mossy pigeon voices in the trees;
the pond all sunk and silent, the lilies wide –
their open yellow eyes,
the long and drawn-out daylight of the day.

A strange moon hoisted then at last
and hanging low above the hill –
a ball of cobwebs in the just blue sky,
a sky that will not quite get dark.

As down below the river slips to find the sea;
the flickering whisper that is left of it –
no breath of wind, the bats going back and forth –
in endless shadow play, in mime.

JOURNEY

I have gone into a landscape
not to come back different
but more myself. It can take days
to go into the hills and listen.

Everything is miles of silence:
a stretch of loch so blue it can't be real,
an eagle floating in the sky,
at night the skies a breath of stars.

I leave behind my loudness
for a time; remember what it means
to swim again, to feel
way out of my depth.

YEARSONG

Green grows the meadow and high sings the curlew,
longer and longer the light;
gentle the river turns slow to the sea,
day after day of pure blue.
A boy climbs high in a pine tree to watch
acres of sky turn to gold;
long hours he waits as the star seeds like pearls
sing out their fires in the night.

One day earth tilts and the light's not the same,
a ripple has shuddered the trees;
auburn and rose touch the hillcrests and glens,
till one after one is on fire.
Apple and pear fall heavy and ripe
with the leaves that are spinning the air.
The days they are restless and searching and wild,
blown by the skirts of the wind.

Silver the river and strong as a salmon,
leaping and turning the rocks.
Lower and lower the deer search the hillsides
as a breath of new snow crests the heights.
The robin is back in the garden once more,
flows out a new song from his heart;
as the earth falls asleep under blankets of white
and the candle of Christmas lights clear.

SONNET

A sonnet is the hardest thing to write:
a little jewellery box of lines that rhyme
and all about one subject: it's a fight
to find the best words and compose in time
the story of a little world – a gift
that will not fade, grow old or lose its power,
no matter what. A sonnet is enough to lift
the heart from what may be the saddest hour;
restore the soul to gladness and to hope,
to let the reader see the day anew
and in a different way. It is a rope
to climb beyond the dark at last and view
the morning rising from the hills of night
in glorious, newborn, precious, amber light.

COLL

I got up long before the dawn;
opened an unlocked door
into a landscape made of moor and loch.
Twelve years old: the only danger barbed wire fences.
I ran until the hillside turned to sand,
and under me the whole Atlantic
softening the white rim of the island
like a sigh. I chased down all the dunes,
barefooting sand so white it might have been
a kind of snow. Sea breathed
in ledges and descents, in many blues
that melded into one. I dared undress
to tread out deep until I lifted
held and unafraid, breath
caught and stolen by the cold.
I entered another world;
melted into something else.
I came out strange and shining, new
and wandered slowly home, the same
yet never quite the same again.

SUMMER

Comes like a barefoot child –
two blue eyes of soft water
and hands like new bread.

There is no wind –
that is what you notice first;
that everything is quiet, that you can hear
the skirl of a boat three miles away,
see the white lip of its leaving across the water.

At midnight the blue will not go away,
is still there, the hills of an island
forty miles north.

Did they go from their black houses also
on these scatterings of June nights;
the women's hands no more than sore and red
after their day in the fields, the home, the shore?

Did they hear the silence too
and waken in the huge blue twilight of the night
to watch the moon hung over the hills in the window?

Maybe it was then they scented
the skin of face, of neck;
remembered the night by the soft sign language
of fingers and wordless tongues.

WESTERN NORWAY

A waterfall in a horse's tail
whitens the lake. A field is ripe with sunlight.

Summer snow still lies
impossibly high. A child

with straw for hair
is learning to walk by falling

in a meadow made of reds and blues.
Her father is building a house

with bare hands,
singing something given him.

KILMARTIN

A day of blue wind;
the first of September and we drove
by headlands and long shores
as light blew in on the land.

Here where they first landed
in boats carved from Ireland;
they came with bare hands,
made clearings out of the woods.

Men who had fashioned the skill
to circle great ledges of stone;
so when moonlight came tilting just sometimes
it poured into perfect place.

Looking back on their lives after all
down the long glens of time;
we see them through mist and perceive them
as minds that had not grown up.

But they steered by night, silent;
learned creeks and the deepest lochs –
traded with far away, learned the language
to buy and sell all they needed.

They whispered flint, the finest knives
tipped for deer and the fear of wolves –
mapmakers, stargazers, settlers –
their stories left in the stone.

A WINTER POEM

On a nothing kind of day in July
I left the grey skies and grey rain,
went into the padded silence of the library
in search of an old story.

I sat at a machine and flickered the screen,
sifted and sifted until I chanced on something –
like finding a flint arrowhead
unearthed beneath my feet.

I was taken back to Greenland and the time of Eric the Red:
how the settlement prospered until it was three thousand strong.
They built a cathedral of red sandstone, a symbol of themselves.
But bit by bit they faltered: they failed to trade with the Inuit,
and the soil was grazed too hard. The ships from Norway dwindled,
disappeared. In the end they must have starved, slowly,
as the ice built its walls about their dying.

The last man was found, face down on a beach,
his blunt and broken knife beside him.

I finished and the computer eye blinked shut.
I went back out into the ice and snow;
the blizzard blinding my day.

BLESSING

October and the geese are back
ragged beyond our windows, voices
torn and sharp. The days grow smaller
as the grey skies turn hurrying and wild –
the heather smoke torn tousled out of chimneys.

But when the light is poured in blessing on the moors
it is Old Testament, and all my labour
and my frail concerns become as nothing
under these great skies left wintering with geese
as frail white snow scatters the morning hills
and this new day is held in light, still,
the coal bucket bumping uselessly my knees
as a curlew mourns the silence miles away
and sunlight, blessed sunlight, fills the eyes
and fills the heart, one moment, then is gone.

ADMISSION

I can never take a photograph of a whole place:
all that is possible is a piece, a part –
there will always be something that is lost, left out.
I could capture the fire with flames dancing the coals,
but not the scent of this small room –
smoke and peat and whisky mixed together;
nor could I turn and take
the whole sea listing and swilling between islands,
or the picture of a tallow-coloured boat
battling across with the low hum of an engine.
I could never catch completely
the skies clearing and the late October light
coming sometimes in a hurrying –
brightness and bleakness
in their play of change for ever.

DONALD ANGUS, HARRIS

Three days beyond his death
they carried him to Luskentyre;
the graves that lie against the sea,
the blue-green breathing of that tide.
The threads in him all left intact;
the woven pattern of the eighty years
to make this place called home –
the love that brought the three strong sons,
that spoke and laughed his Gaelic;
the knowledge of the rise and fall of psalms –
the sung wave that underheld the hand,
carried high the sureness of the heart.
All this they brought that day and buried there
beside the vastness of the inblown sea,
to sleep against the light of Luskentyre.

AFTER CULLODEN

The wounded wandered home in Gaelic
by rivers and back roads;
all they had fought for
unsure and broken.

How long before they saw
their language and their land
like a limb that's tied too tight;
still there but dying all the time.

Or like a wildcat caught at last –
not killed, but tamed;
de-clawed, castrated –
then stroked and told to purr.

THE BAY AT THE BACK OF THE OCEAN

I come back here brittle and broken,
to be washed up new and rinsed and clean,
with eyes that no longer see
the clutter of what must be done.

To be made pure west again
on days the sea's moiling and searching,
roaring over beaches in chariots,
beneath the battlefield of the skies.

Then when the light comes, sometimes,
shimmering like a whole shoal of herring,
and the wind stands still, I think –
this is to fill the heart.

WOODVILLE

And I remember, father, how you found my room
to read me stories and to smooth my pillow
when asthma filled me so that breathing seemed
a fight to climb a hill.
It was the middle of the night; you brought a book
and read until it gentled me to sleep.

I think of how your brother once upon a time
had heaved and stretched for breath the same:
I wonder if you'd learned to find him too
and kept your voice as easy and untroubled as for me.
I only wish that I could find you somewhere in the dark
to tell you all this later what it meant.

DESPITE THE DARK

Sometimes it is not strange to think that God
is out behind the darkness of the night;
that there is hope, however small and odd
the thought might be. Sometimes it is all right
believing that the good will yet win out
against the weight of hate, and that the light
will shine again when all the voices doubt
and you have fought the dark with all your might.
Lift up your hand and see its grace anew
and open wide the window to the dawn
to hear the birds that sing the morning in.
For this is still a thousand times more true
than fear and lies and giving in to wrong.
So keep your faith – believe, begin again.

JANET'S BEACH

When you take the last bit of hill
over from Kilninver to the Isle of Seil,
you pass a road end that vanishes
down through dwarf birches to the sea
and a white beach of sand, blue water.

It was by the Bridge over the Atlantic
they found your car, Janet, and you gone.
Once upon a time you'd lived in the house
at the bottom of that track.

I like to think that once you left your car
and gave up your struggle against the dark
by going back to the water,
the light into which you grew showed you
a house that you had never known before;
its welcome waiting at the track's end,
and the beach beautiful beyond –
made of more grains of good
than you could ever count.

THE HEALING

That's all I know:
her eyes were broken and he mended them.
When he held her head
she said it was as though
the light crept back into them;
as though the sun opened over her shoulders
and made the morning new.
She was mended all right,
but not just her sight –
the way she saw the world.

TRAVELLERS

Once I saw them coming for a funeral;
blown in on a wild day, women mostly,
hugging themselves against the slanting rain.

Travellers, I thought. And I realised I was afraid,
knowing them as little
as the prodigal son his own brother.
We come from the same country
yet speak different tongues –
grown apart and strange, wary of the other.

Yet I believe these are the ones
Christ would have visited had it been here
and not the hot, olive fields of Galilee he walked.
He'd have gone to river camps
to share the laughter of summer pearls
and in the long, blue June nights
they'd have shared kindness and stories.

What are they now but the last broken fragments
of a beautiful vessel that held pure water?

ARK

Forty days the thunder grey of skies;
the breathing of a sea that never was before.

Each day the ship they'd built
heaved and juddered over a shoreless tide,
a darkness receding forever.

Then, one midnight, something like light:
a lessening, a moment's opening, a window.

In the morning the crystal glitter of birdsong;
the broken silence of a coast.

THE DEER

Only now I think how they came down
that morning through the dark to stand and watch
my going after eight years there; the careful eyes,
the heads bent forwards, and I remembered then
the winters I went out to feed the furry mouths –
those frozen months when nothing broke the ground
but snow and still more snow, the earth like stone;
when they slipped soft and shy from out the wood
and anything I found I fed them with my hands.
That dawn I think they knew that I was going for good.
As though they came to say some strange farewell.

THE BURREN

Here on the sheer edge of the Atlantic
a ledge, a shelf, on the last west of Ireland
out of limestone, the singing of water.

Little crevices of flowers blow, moments of laughter,
fists of defiance raised against temples
chiselled by wind.

Yet listen, lie down,
put your ear soft to a ground
older than time.

Hear the water note of the curlew, her crying,
the woven gold of a skylark's threads,
the dark scar of the raven.

The ones who grew here first, the men
who skilled flint to fine tips, who lived
under these huge and empty skies

they have turned to limestone too, their lichened skulls
have curled back into all they came from –
fossil stories of a fragile light.

SALT

When you have forgotten what it means
to have the wind hurrying your window all night long
it's time to find the island. There is a gate –
beyond, a track that's made of sand
winding down the machair. You'll hear the sea
long before you're there, or the shoulders of the island
have opened so that all the horses of the west
are galloping the beach, again and now again.
And if you should open too and let in light,
it is because the breakages within you are so many
and the salt, no matter how it hurts, will heal.

LISTEN

Walk the evening's scent in May
after thunder has fluttered the clouds
and rain, gentle as petals,
turns the garden to a green goblet.

Stand then at the garden's heart
and listen still to droplets in the trees
as even in the last light's edge
a bee nudges blossom to blossom.

FALL

I went out with a long stick to knock the last damsons down.
Most of them had fallen, just a few clung to branches;
their lovely velvet skin a marbled blue, the colour of dark lips.

The wind came to hush the high branches;
I slashed with the stick and hard they came down –
heavy drops of damsons into the soft ground,
and I carried the basket up and back to the house.

I carried it inside as the sun like a tipped over thing
spilled a last time, to set alight me, the trees, the fields
in a bonfire of yellows and reds.

TAY

At the far end of the river
it grows into a wide whiteness:

the hills on the other side
long and blue and distant.

Here on the northern rim
the jostle and hum of city

never sleeping, rummaging restless;
the bright jewellery of the streets,

the stacks of high-rise flats,
bracelets of bridges

and beyond
a place where sweet grows salt –

where there's nothing on the edge of the sky
but a thin line of silence.

BIRTHING

We are brought out of love
into a world sore to the touch:
it hurts, but it is worth it.

HELEN

I'll always know that I will find you
after Mull and the wandering of the road,
beneath the grey head of the ben,
beside a sea gone wild.

Until the island lying still at anchor,
at the day's end then at last:
air full of fish, the stink of peat –
and the promise of a whisky on the other side.

WWW.IONABOOKS.COM

The Iona Community was founded in Glasgow in 1938 by George MacLeod, minister, visionary and prophetic witness for peace, in the context of the poverty and despair of the Depression. Its original task of rebuilding the monastic ruins of Iona Abbey became a sign of hopeful rebuilding of community in Scotland and beyond. Today, we are about 250 Members, mostly in Britain, and 1500 Associate Members, with 1400 Friends worldwide. Together and apart, 'we follow the light we have, and pray for more light'.

For information on the Iona Community contact:
The Iona Community, 21 Carlton Court, Glasgow G5 9JP, UK.
Phone: 0141 429 7281
e-mail: admin@iona.org.uk; web: www.iona.org.uk

For enquiries about visiting Iona, please contact:
Iona Abbey, Isle of Iona, Argyll PA76 6SN, UK. Phone: 01681 700404
e-mail: enquiries@iona.org.uk